SMOOTHIES FOR WELLNESS AND

50+ AMAZING SMOOTHIE RECIPES INSPIRED BY THE ALKALINE, PALEO, MACROBIOTIC, AND MEDITERRANEAN DIETS

By Marta Tuchowska

Copyright Marta Tuchowska© 2014, 2016

www.HolisticWellnessProject.com

All rights reserved. No part of this publication may be reproduced, stored in a retrieval system, or transmitted, in any form or by any means, electronic, mechanical, photocopying, recording, or otherwise, without the prior written permission of the author and the publishers.

The scanning, uploading, and distribution of this book via the Internet or via any other means without the permission of the author is illegal and punishable by law. Please purchase only authorized electronic editions, and do not participate in or encourage electronic piracy of copyrighted materials.

INTRODUCTION

It all starts on a cellular level—**a healthy and vibrant body**, as well as a **focused mind**.

Oriental medicine teaches people how to take care of themselves, as it recognizes the importance of prevention. It's all about getting **committed to health**. Oriental medicine doctors make it their mission to teach people more about **proper self-care**. It's as easy as that.

Think about it as **the best time investment** that you can possibly make.

Unfortunately, Western medicine relies, in most cases, on **quick fixes**.

The reason why I am writing my **wellness books** is that I want my readers to realize that taking care of oneself in a holistic way is fun. I am also dedicated to **creating my holistic wellness lifestyle** that can be the example to others. I don't want to be a preaching guru. I want to show others what I do on a daily basis, and hopefully, motivate them and inspire them. Choosing a wellness lifestyle and making a decision to **seek balance** (yes, I am a seeker!) in a holistic way, was the best thing I have done for myself. Now, I want to spread **the word of wellness**.

What's the biggest obstacle that modern people in the 21st century are facing? **LACK OF ENERGY**! Yes...with no energy there is no zest for life. It's not only your body that gets lazy, but also your mind. It's easy to get suckered in by the vicious cycle of just feeling awful all the time. The emotions are out of control, and our wellness is gone. Sounds familiar? I am sure it does; everyone has been there. That's the price for a fast-paced lifestyle that many people are paying in this day and age.

The best thing you can do now, is to start taking better care of yourself. Yes, I know--easier said than done...After all, everyone is always so pressed for time.

I am a busy person myself. I am very active, and I also have lots of professional projects going on. I also recognize the fact that the times are financially demanding and stressful.

But what do I do; where do I start?

I know that I just have to invest some time in my health. If there is no health, there is nothing...I am not referring to just feeling OK, or going to see your doc to get a checkup and getting the results that say that everything is great (of course, it is great, and you should visit your doc for some examinations every now and then, but this is not the ultimate goal here).

We want **HOLISTIC HEALTH**! Infinite energy levels, focused and creative mind, feeling amazing in your body, setting an example for other people, and spreading the word of wellness...When you get there, you will start attracting better relationships and even career opportunities. You will feel better, you will look better, and quite naturally, you will attract some really awesome circumstances into your life.

A few years ago, I decided I needed some drastic changes in my life, and I started working on my body and eating healthy. I knew I had no choice; I wanted high energy levels. I began paying closer attention to what I was eating and took interest in **the alkaline diet**.

If you have never heard of the alkaline diet/lifestyle before, I suggest you download this free eBook with recipes and charts so that you can easily understand and apply this concept for optimal health:

Download link:

www.holisticwellnessproject.com/alkaline

My biggest obstacle was to quit coffee. It's such a stupid drug really! I knew that it was **against my alkaline lifestyle,** and that it was making me tired even though I wasn't drinking that much of it.

In the morning, I would have my mega cup of coffee, and even though I was eating healthy, a few hours later, around lunch time I would get a big headache that would just carry on the whole afternoon. I also needed a regular nap in the afternoon. I knew that I was wasting my time, hitting the sack way too much. I also knew that coffee was to blame, and that I had to reduce it or find some other way. In other words—coffee was taking my energy away; it was cutting me off my high energy levels! This is why I turned to smoothies and discovered a new world, which I got addicted to and got my energy back.

Ok, I am not telling you to quit coffee; maybe you are not as sensitive as I am. I am just trying to inspire you to turn to **healthier alternatives** that will work for you and for your **optimal health** in the long run. If you are a big coffee lover, just try to reduce it for some time, and see what happens.

Now, I use caffeine only occasionally, more as a special treat, not as an addiction (trust me, a few years back, I was a caffeine-addict!).

I like green tea, and as you will see, I use it in my smoothies as well.

Once in a while, I have a coffee (organic) with some almond milk—actually, it's more like almond milk with some coffee. But I usually choose a smoothie, as I know that it's REAL ENERGY that it gives me. I want something highly nutritious.

From time to time, I use coffee with almond milk as a base for my smoothies, so if you are a coffee lover, no worries, there is a simple way to gradually reduce your coffee intake and make a gradual transition towards smoothies. If you have already reduced or quit coffee or simply never been into drinking it or abusing it—congratulations! Thanks to this book, you will be able to expand your healthy smoothie recipes.

In the winter, I like black tea from time to time, especially chai tea, as I love all those Indian spices, and I figured out how to use it for my smoothies as well. I sometimes use yogi tea, which is basically like chai tea, but with no black tea, and so no caffeine in it.

If you are not caffeine-sensitive, some tiny amounts are fine. I like to balance it with highly nutritious smoothies. I don't know if you realize, but caffeine, especially coffee and black tea, deprives our body of magnesium, iron, and many other vital minerals. Hence, the lack of energy in the long run. This is why I am bringing up the topic of coffee and caffeine.

I must admit that I like experimenting with healthy foods in general, smoothies can be extremely creative, and I hope that my book will get you hooked on them and encourage you to create your own.

This morning, for example, I got up and realized that my kitchen shelves were almost empty. I only had 2 oranges, 1 lemon, some oats, and a mix of algae. What did I do? A smoothie, yes I blended orange-lemon juice with a half-cup of soaked oats with cinnamon and about 2 tablespoons of soaked algae nori and wakame. I got my physical and mental energy immediately! In fact, I just got back from almost an hour run followed by some gentle yoga, a cold shower, and a healthy breakfast (kale salad wraps with avocados, almonds, and tomatoes). Now, I am writing this new book and feeling extremely focused and happy. Like the "here and now" feeling. I call it "the natural high". I finally found my drug, which is **wellness**.

This book is for everyone who wants to feel amazing in his or her body. Whether you are a stay-at-home mom, a wellness nut, a business owner, or a busy employee—you will find something for yourself. If you are a student and are looking for a focused mind—you have just found your book.

Smoothies are so easy to make, it only takes a few minutes! You don't need a super expensive blender (of course, I wish I had one of those!). The one I am using now is something between poor and mediocre, but it does its job for the time being.

Back to our wellness goals:

Whatever it is that you want to achieve, whether it is:

-Weight loss

-More energy levels

-Better memory

-Better sleep

-More zest for life

-Better digestion

-More stamina and vitality

You need more nutrients in your body.

Since I follow the alkaline diet and I care about the 70/30 rule, I can assure you that my recipes are usually alkalizing, from mildly alkalizing to super alkalizing.

Even if you are new to **the Alkaline Diet**, if you start on my recipes, and you start experiencing higher energy levels in your body, you will be naturally motivated to do more. So, do the first step now--get yourself a nice smoothie.

Most of my recipes are Paleo friendly, for those of you guys who are Paleo. I sometimes use grains like quinoa in my smoothies (I know! Not Paleo...), if you feel like it can damage your Paleo lifestyle, then just skip those ingredients (I suggest you try it though, integral, unprocessed grains are not bad for you, I am sure that our digestive track has adapted in the Neolithic era..)

A few more words on Paleo:

This is my personal opinion on Paleo. I like the idea of getting back to the roots, as well as eating organic, unprocessed foods. Fresh fruits and vegetables, nuts, algae, fish, and meat (organic of course!), as well as some decent physical activity, this is a true Paleolithic lifestyle. Now, I do Paleo part-time. Why? First of all, I am not a big meat lover...

What I like about the Paleo Diet is the creativity that preparing Paleo-friendly desserts and smoothies involve. I find it fascinating. Hence, my booklet is also inspired by Paleo.

Then, I am a truly **alkaline girl**. But I also recognize that many alkaline lovers go too strict on themselves, I have met some people who were starving themselves to death or doing some weird green cleanses even though, I am quite sure, they did not know if they needed one. The Alkaline lifestyle is better made by first choosing organic, unprocessed foods, proper hydration, and making about 70% of your diet alkaline foods, and the remaining 30% acidic. Of course, there are different kinds of acidic foods. Not all acidic foods are bad. Some foods are mildly acidic, and some are extremely acidic. For example, a banana is an acidifying fruit. However, it is better for you than a processed cake, I hope you get the comparison.

Ok, some charts may vary as for bananas PH. Many alkaline gurus say that bananas are 25% sugar, and so as a consumed food, it becomes acidifying in our system. However, they are also rich in potassium, which is an alkaline mineral.

This is why I am not against bananas. I am not that alkaline strict. I like finding balance in everything I do.

I love bananas in my before and after workout smoothies. If, for some reason, you are against bananas, or some sort of medical condition tells you not to eat them, that's fine. I am just trying to show two sides of the coin and encourage you to make your own decision.

Create your own bandwagon and be the driver!

This is what I do!

I also like the **Mediterranean Diet**. As a general rule, it is based on integral cereals, plenty of fresh fruits and vegetables, fish, and seafood, some amount of white meat, and limited red meat or no red meat. This is the real Mediterranean Diet. However, since I have been living in Spain for about eight years now, and have also lived in Italy for about a year, let me tell you that I have only met very few people who practice a truly balanced Mediterranean Diet. The most common mistake that they do is that they overindulge in fried foods and white bread, rice, and other unhealthy carbs (yes, not the good carbs I was praising before).

What do I like about the Mediterranean Diet? The relaxed lifestyle, and the way the Southern Europeans enjoy life and make eating something like a special ritual. Fresh salads, fruits, juices, good oils like olive oil..

I also love the **Macrobiotic Diet**. I will surely write a book on it, but for now, lesson number 1, learn to use algae in your diet.

This diet helped to cure my eye from uveitis (combined with homeopathy, something that I mention in my BIO).

Algae, sesame seeds, integral cereal, and some occasional tofu—my cooking is also inspired by the **Macrobiotic Diet**.

The reason why I mention all these diets is to encourage you to make your own choices; this is what I think, you may disagree. This is what works for me, it may not work for you. This is where so many gurus go wrong; they are telling you what to do.

I am telling you to brainstorm and **create your own experiences with diets**, and as a result, **your own holistic lifestyle**. What works for me may not work for you. This is why I wanted to create a smoothie recipes book that everyone can benefit from, also those who are on some specific kind of bandwagon. If you like where the bandwagon is taking you, admire the view and stay there. Just make sure it does work for you.

Energy and vibrant health—this is what **creative smoothies** will provide you with.

Of course, smoothies are not the ultimate cure. They form a part of a wellness lifestyle that you will get addicted to...

Here are some ingredients that I use in my smoothies:

-Fruits

-Veggies

-Vegan milk: almond milk (highly alkaline), rice milk, sometimes some soy milk (GMO free of course)

-Filtered water

-Herbal infusions

-Fresh lemon juice, orange juice or grapefruit juice

-Powdered nuts and dried fruits

-All kinds of algae—leaves or powdered (for example, powdered chlorella or spiruline, wakame, nori...)

-Soy lecithin granules—in moments of stress and mental fatigue, as well as physical recovery (you may want to consult a naturopathic doctor, it is a natural supplement, but should be taken periodically)

-Cooled green tea, and sometimes black tea and coffee (only occasionally)

-Cooked quinoa, brown rice, amaranth, and millet—I like using some leftovers in my smoothies, if not, why not?

-Herbs and spices, especially for smoothies like Spanish gazpacho or salmonejo; so tasty...great for the summer...!

-Coconut oil and olive oil

By simply adding one smoothie a day to your routine, you will find yourself nicely energized and willing to do some more healthy stuff.

If you already are a wellness freak, then I am sure that you will find some new ideas for your smoothies.

If you want to lose weight—focus on nutrients, this is what your body needs. Do you know what puts weight on people? Unhealthy food in exaggerated amounts, fast food and processed foods are full of chemicals and drugs to make us hooked on them.

There are only empty calories and no nutrients; this is why our body is always hungry, hence the binging, way too much snacking, and gaining weight.

Then, there are the fad diets, low fat, low calorie, and again, it's all processed food…it's so sad what we have done to ourselves…now it's time to get back to something healthy and reap the health benefits that we all deserve…

Why do I talk about high energy levels so much?

Easy—life is short; I prefer to take advantage of all the amazing things that it brings instead of feeling like I was run over by a bulldozer every morning…

I also believe that feeling good can help you attract all other great things into your life, whether it's travelling, finances, or relationships.

So...prepare your blender and a shopping list, we have some serious work to do...

Now, it's time to nicely and smoothly dive into my smooth smoothie world.

Enjoy!

DISCLAIMER

The author of this book is not a doctor and it is not her intention to claim that the treatments described in this book can be a substitute for professional medical advice or any standard medical treatments. Her aim is to simply present certain alternative and holistic therapies that can be applied at home.

All the information in this book has been carefully researched and checked for factual accuracy. However, the author and publishers make no warranty, expressed or implied, that the information contained herein is appropriate for every individual, situation or purpose and assume no responsibility for errors or omission. The reader assumes the risk and full responsibility for all actions.

JOIN MY FREE ALKALINE WELLNESS NEWSLETTER

Join my wellness + holistic lifestyle newsletter and get free instant
access to my guide: "Revolutionize Your Life with Alkaline Foods" + my insider news, tons of super healthy recipes sent to you for free on a regular basis +amazing free bonuses + receive all my upcoming books for free or 99c.
Start creating a happy body, mind and spirit today!

Subscribe here: www.HolisticWellnessProject.com/alkaline

I hope to see you there!

If you have any technical problems with your free download, email us at:

info@holisticwellnessproject.com

We are here to help!

RECIPE #1 Green Tea Mix

This is a great recipe if you are sleepy and really need some caffeine but don't want to get too anxious. Green tea is full of antioxidants and acts as a mild stimulant. I recommend it if you want to reduce coffee.

I was trying to introduce my friend to green tea, but she hated it. I prepared this smoothie for her, and now she loves it. The smoothie will taste sweet and delicious thanks to bananas! This is why I recommend it to those who would like to benefit from green tea, yet can't stand its taste (another option is to get some green tea powder in capsules).

Serves: 1-2

Ingredients:

- 1 cup of cooled green tea
- Fresh juice of 1 orange
- 1 avocado (peel, remove the pit, slice)
- 1 teaspoon of chlorella powder
- 1 banana (or more, depends on you and your body!)
- A few strawberries
- Half cup of raw almond milk

Instructions:

Brew some green tea first. If you are pressed for time, here's what I recommend: prepare half-cup of your green tea (hot but not boiling water), leave in for a few minutes, and then fill the remaining half-cup with some cold water. This is how you can obtain cooled green tea immediately.Blend with other ingredients, and serve immediately.

Garnish with a cinnamon stick. So delicious!

RECIPE #2 Pink is Sweet!

Let's go pink! Here comes a smoothie for Barbie doll fans...

Serves: 1-2

Ingredients:

- 1 cup of blueberries
- 1 cup of raspberries
- Half avocado
- 1 cup of vegan milk (soy milk, rice milk, hazelnut milk—if you use soy milk, make sure it's GMO free)
- Half tablespoon of soy lecithin
- Some powdered nuts (I like almond powder)

Instructions:

1. Wash the blueberries and raspberries.

2. Wash and peel the avocado, remove pit, cut in half.

3. Blend all the ingredients. Serve slightly chilled with some raisins and nuts. Garnish with a slice of avocado!

I recommend this smoothie for students.

It's great for breakfasts or afternoon snacks.

For more energy and concentration, I recommend some powdered almonds that use can squeeze in.

OPTIONAL:

- If your kid does not want to drink this smoothie, add some cocoa powder. Make it choco-delicious!

RECIPE #3 Super Alkaline

This one is super alkaline and green. It may take a while until you get used to it.

Whenever I feel like I can't concentrate, I have a headache, or lack energy, I resort to this **alkaline green power**!

Creativity is the key to alkalinity. Alkalinity is delicious and fun!

Serves: 2

Ingredients:

-1 big avocado

-1 cup of steamed and chopped broccoli (Yes, broccoli in the smoothie!)

-A handful of baby spinach

-1 tablespoon of powdered spiruline

-2 glasses of raw almond milk or rice milk

-1 teaspoon of cinnamon

- Juice of one lemon

-Juice of one grapefruit

Instructions:

1. Wash the spinach, lemon, grapefruit, and other ingredients.
2. Squeeze one lemon and one grapefruit.

3. Mix the juice with other ingredients. Blend. Serve with some cinnamon and raisins for taste.

Enjoy!

This is going to be a massive green smoothie, so you may want to share it with someone.

RECIPE #4 Anti-cold Smoothie

This smoothie is great for winter time. You can also use it to strengthen your immune system and prevent colds and flu.

Serves: 1-2

Ingredients:

- Half cup of Indian chai tea with spices (I buy it in teabags, it is a mix of black tea and spices like cardamom, clove, ginger, cinnamon, and pepper).
- Half cup of vegan milk (almond, coconut etc.)
- 1 teaspoon of cinnamon
- Half clove of garlic
- 1 tablespoon of ginger (finely chopped)
- 1 banana
- 1 avocado

Instructions:

1. Prepare some chai tea and set aside.

2. Wash the avocado and banana. Peel and cut.

3. Blend all the ingredients and enjoy! Chai tea contains some black tea, if you are caffeine sensitive, replace with a simple yoga tea with spices (it has no theine).

As for milk—follow your own preferences. I like all kinds of vegan milk, but sometimes, I also use goat's milk. I don't drink cow's milk. Check out what works for you, and make your own choice.

RECIPE #5 Easy Summer Smoothie

This smoothie is really refreshing! Great for hot summers!

Serves: 1-2

Ingredients:

- 2 peaches (remove the pit, of course)
- 1 cup of cherries (these need to be pitted of course)
- About 1 cup of finely chopped watermelon (so refreshing! Help yourself, and snack some when you are making this smoothie!)
- Juice of 2 oranges
- 1 teaspoon of powdered chlorella

Instructions:

Blend all the ingredients and enjoy. Serve slightly chilled. You may want to garnish it with some fresh mint or rosemary herb!

RECIPE #6 Anti-cellulite

I recommend this smoothie as a natural energy booster, especially in the summer. If you suffer from sluggish circulation, slow bowel movement, water retention, or cellulite, try to drink it every day or at least 3 times a week.

Serves: 1-2

Ingredients:

- 1 cup of cooled horsetail infusion (use 1-2 teabags)
- 1 grapefruit
- 1 lemon
- 1 cup of blueberries
- 1 apple
- 1 peach
- Handful of baby spinach or kale salad
- Half teaspoon of spiruline powder

Instructions:
1. Prepare 1 cup of horsetail infusion (use 1-2 teabags) and set aside to cool down.
2. In the meantime, wash and peel other ingredients and cut into small pieces.
3. Mix the horsetail infusion with other ingredients; you may also add some ice cubes. Blend. Add more water or aloe vera water if needed.
4. Add some spiruline powder, and stir energetically.
5. Serve immediately, enjoy!

RECIPE #7 Sweet Dreams

Can't sleep at night?

Make sure you don't go to bed too hungry, but of course, don't overeat.

Everyone knows this rule. How to put theory into practice? A tasty and relaxing smoothie is a great solution!

Serves:1

Ingredients:

-half cup of soaked oats

-1 banana

-1 glass of oat milk (or other milk of your choice)

-2 teaspoons of raw cocoa powder

-1 teaspoon of coconut oil

-Half teaspoon of cinnamon

Instructions:

1. Soak about half cup of oats with some warm water. Set aside.
2. Wash, peel, and cut the banana, mix with oats, oat milk, and blend.
3. Add 1 teaspoon of coconut oil, cocoa powder and cinnamon. Stir energetically for about a minute.
4. Serve immediately, enjoy, relax and sleep like a baby!

RECIPE #8 Anti-cellulite Again!

Here is another variation of the recipe #6.

Serves:2

Ingredients:

- 2 cups of chopped pineapple
- 1 cup of cooled green tea
- 1 orange
- A handful of spinach
- 1 cup of chopped melon
- Half cup of raw almond milk
- A few leaves of fresh mint

Instructions:

Blend all the ingredients. You can garnish with some cinnamon powder. This is a really nice, alkaline smoothie with some powerful anti-cellulite properties!

RECIPE #9 I like it sweet!

Ok, so your kid does not like fruits/ veggies?

How about trying this amazing smoothie?

My tip: don't tell him /her that it contains some spinach and alga wakame...

Serves:1-2

Ingredients:

- 1 cup of raw almond milk or rice milk
- 4 teaspoons of raw cacao powder
- 1 tablespoon of raisins
- Handful of spinach
- A few raspberries
- 1 banana
- 1 teaspoon of organic honey

If your kid is active and sporty, I suggest you also add some soaked oats to give him/her more energy!

Instructions:

Blend and enjoy. You may want to serve it with some nuts. Superman's food!

RECIPE #10 Food Cravings!

My holistic nutrition teacher, would always tell us that the best thing to fight sugar cravings is to have a tablespoon of coconut oil. I have always stuck to this tip, and it has worked great for me.

I think that there is no reason to fight anything, as long as you prepare something that tastes sweet and is also healthy. You can treat yourself to something delicious and really good for you at the same time.

This smoothie also makes sure that your body will be given plenty of minerals, vitamins, and nutrients.

Uncontrolled food cravings very often come from a lack of those important nutrients. Our body says: feed me, feed me, I am still hungry!!! This smoothie will keep your body well fed, and so your mind won't be asking you for any unhealthy foods...

Serves: 1

Ingredients:

- 1 cup of cooled roibosh tea
- 1 cup of rice milk or raw almond milk
- 1 avocado (peeled and pitted)
- 1 tablespoon of coconut oil
- 1 cucumber
- 1 apple

Instructions:

1. Prepare one cup of roibosh tea (1-2 teabags), and let it cool down.
2. In the meantime, wash and peel the avocado, cucumber, and apple. Chop.
3. Mix with cooled roibosh tea and the rest of the ingredients, and blend.

Enjoy!

If you still find yourself craving something sweet, have a few slices of apple with some almond butter or peanut butter☺. In the winter, it might be an awesome idea to bake it slightly with some powdered cinnamon.

OPTIONAL:

If you lack energy, add one teaspoon of soy lecithin granules or spiruline power.

RECIPE # 11 Spanish Gazpacho Inspiration

I love Spanish gazpacho! Here's my version of "gazpaching".

I have transformed the original recipe a bit to make it even healthier!

Serves:2

Ingredients:

- 3 cucumbers
- 6 tomatoes
- 2 red peppers
- Fresh juice of 1 lemon
- 1 pinch of Himalaya salt (or a bit more, depends on your preferences. You may add more salt later when gazpacho is made).
- 2 tablespoon of olive oil
- 1 tablespoon of balsamic vinegar
- 2 pinches of black pepper (powered)
- 1 onion
- 2 carrots
- 1 cup of water (filtered)
- 2 cloves of garlic
- 1 cup of sweet almond milk (raw, unsweetened)
- Alga wakame (cut out about 3 square centimeters, or, just cut out something that more or less resembles a size of an average cookie)

Instructions:

1. In a small utensil, soak wakame in some cold water (filtered). Cover, and keep for about 15 mins. In the meantime...

2. Wash and peel all the veggies, including tomatoes (I usually soak them in some hot-boiling water so that the peel comes out)
3. Chop the onions and garlic and the rest of the veggies.
4. Blend all the ingredients including algae. Add more water if needed.

Serve cold. Add salt, rosemary or fresh basil to taste.

MY TIP:

I buy algae mix: there is some wakame, nori, agar-agar, and I just take a couple of tablespoons and soak them in water and add them to my salads, soups, and smoothies.

RECIPE12 # Spanish Salmorejo Inspiration

Here comes another recipe inspired by Spanish cuisine. Of course, I transformed it slightly.

Both gazpacho and salmorejo are native to Andalucía which is south of Spain. Summers can be incredibly hot there, hence the refreshing and nourishing summer recipes like creams and soups.

Serves:2-3

Ingredients:

- 2 slices of toasted bread (integral, gluten-free)
- 2 garlic cloves
- 10 ripe tomatoes
- 100 ml of virgin olive oil
- About 3-4 square centimeters of alga nori (cut it out from the leave)
- Handful of spinach
- 1 cup of water
- 2 tablespoons of balsamic vinegar
- Himalaya salt (1-2 pinches) and black pepper

Instructions:

1. Soak alga nori in some filtered water and leave in for 10-15 minutes.

2. In the meantime, peel the tomatoes and garlic. Wash spinach.

3. Cut the bread into small pieces.

Blend all the ingredients including alga nori. Serve cold. Season with some salt and black pepper according to your preferences.

Traditionally, it is served with some hard-boiled eggs (cooled). It's up to you if you want it as a smoothie or a soup.

RECIPE13 #Thirsty!

One of my friends wanted to do the alkaline diet, but her main obstacle was to force herself to get more hydration; she hated drinking water! At the same time, she was addicted to soft drinks and other artificial smoothies.

Luckily, I managed to get her hooked on this recipe. Once she began to experience the basic effects of alkalinity, she wanted to do more and more. Now, she drinks enough water to float away, just like me!

This is an excellent, watery-like smoothie that I recommend for those who can't stand the original taste of our good, old H_2O.

Serves:1-2

Ingredients:

- One quarter of fresh watermelon, chopped (remove the seeds before blending)
- A few slices of pineapple
- A juice of one grapefruit
- 1 cucumber
- 2 glasses of water
- 1 tablespoon of organic honey

Instructions:

1. Wash the watermelon, pineapple, grapefruit, and cucumber. Remove the peel and chop
2. Squeeze the grapefruit juice
3. Blend all the ingredients, and mix the smoothie with more water (about 1 liter).

This is how you are going to obtain a really delicious, tasty, and re-mineralizing water that will help you quit all those unhealthy chemical drinks.

Serve cold with some fresh mint and ice cubes.

So refreshing!!!

RECIPE14 #Minerals

This smoothie is a great mix of natural minerals that your body needs to put you back in vibrant health.

I love it after strenuous workouts, especially in the summer!

Serves:1-2

Ingredients:

- 1 cup of cooled roibosh tea
- 1 cup of cooled kukicha tea (three years's tea)
- 1 cucumber
- 1 banana
- Juice of 1 lemon
- Handful of spinach

Instructions:

1. Prepare some roibosh tea and kukicha tea, to cool them down just add some ice cubes or cold water (only when the tea is brewed)
2. In the meantime, wash and peel other ingredients (no need to peel the spinach, right?)
3. Squeeze 1 lemon

Now, mix all the ingredients, including your freshly squeezed lemon juice.

You can also add some ice cubes. Personally, I am not a big fan of super cold drinks, but it's up to you and your preferences. My recipes should be only the starting point for you.

OPTIONAL:

Add one teaspoon of powdered chlorella (which reminds me that it's time for my chlorella smoothie now).

One more thing, I really recommend this smoothie for females. Like I said in the intro, coffee depletes us of many vital minerals, including iron. Since we are the ones, who for some reason, were created to suffer once a month (do I need to state how?), we are especially prone to iron deficiency.

My tip is—even if you can't live without coffee or black tea, at least abstain from it while on your period. Make sure you include foods and drinks that are rich in iron as well as other minerals. You will also have more energy levels and feel less moody (or you might not experience mood swings at all), so your partner will be happier as well. Just my tip, lol!

RECIPE15 #Super Breakfast

This is a really energizing smoothie that makes sure that you are all ready to go and smash it with your fitness goals!

Serves: 1-2

Ingredients:

- 2 bananas
- 1 kiwi
- 1 apple
- 1 cup of vegan milk (I like rice milk or sweet almond milk, but can be also good quality soy milk*)
- 1 cup of cooked brown rice or cooked quinoa (might be a good idea to use some leftovers from your dinner)
- 1 teaspoon of spiruline powder
- Juice of 2 grapefruits
- A few leaves of kale

Instructions:

1. Wash all the fruits

2. Peel the kiwis and bananas, you can leave the apple unpeeled, it's up to you. Cut to pieces (depends on your blender preferences…)

3. Squeeze grapefruit juice.

4. Blend all the ingredients, and enjoy your workout!

RECIPE16 # Detox

If you want to detoxify, here comes a great and easy recipe for you.

Serves:1

Ingredients:

- 1 cup of green tea (cooled)
- Some fresh mint leaves
- 2 Carrots
- 2 Apples
- 1 teaspoon of cinnamon
- 1 celery stalk (chopped)
- Half cup of rice milk

Instructions:

1. Brew some green tea, don't make it too strong. Cool it down by adding some ice cubes
2. Wash and peel the carrots, apples, and celery stalk.

Blend all the ingredients and enjoy!

If you are theine sensitive and can't even drink green tea, replace it with some theine free tea, for example roibosh or kukicha. Mint tea would be great as well! You could also mix green tea with some mint tea (hmm...shall I write a book on teas...?)

RECIPE #17 Vitamin C Party

Why do we need vitamin C?

It's pretty obvious for most of us—it takes care of our immune system, prevents colds and flus, and makes us stronger.

Vitamin C is also of paramount importance to:

- Eye health
- Cardiovascular health, circulation
- Cancer and stroke prevention
- Natural anti-age treatments (let's face the truth, we are all bond to age, however a healthy and balanced diet can make a difference and tell those wrinkles to take it easy!)

A word of caution…

There are plenty of vitamin supplements available on the market. I am not against them, however, very often, people buy them and use them "on their own account" without consulting their doctor first. My way of thinking is: do you really need to take those artificial vitamins? Is it really necessary for your case?

I am a big fan of naturopathy, this is why I use smoothies that provide me with all vitamins and minerals naturally. Of course, I go to see my doc every now and then, and I get a blood test done to see if everything is OK.

The problem is that many people don't. My tip for you is—don't self-medicate with artificial vitamins. And, if for some reason it is recommended for your case, or your doctor tells you so, make sure you pick up the reliable brand.

Now, back to NATURAL!

Serves:1-2

Ingredients:

- 2 tomatoes
- 2 kiwis
- Fresh juice of 2 oranges
- 1 cup of water
- 1 cup of green broccoli, steamed

Instructions:

1. Wash the ingredients
2. Peel the tomatoes and kiwis
3. Squeeze fresh orange juice, and mix it with 1 cup of water
4. Blend with other ingredients and enjoy!
Serve immediately!

More on vitamins:
Back in the 90ties, when I was a kid, there was a big vitamin C craze going on. I would take my vitamin C supplements daily, yet, I was always ill!
Luckily, my parents resorted to naturopathy. They never believed in all those trends.

RECIPE #18 Smoothie Ice-Cream

This recipe can be both a smoothie, or you can take it to a whole new level and make some delicious ice-cream! It is Paleo friendly and vegan friendly as well.

Serves:1-2

Ingredients:

- 2 ripe avocados
- 1 cup of rice milk or almond milk
- A few tablespoons of raw cacao powder
- 2 teaspoons of organic honey (ok, you got me here, not too sure if paleos eat honey...!)

Instructions:

1. Wash and peel the avocados, remove the seed.
2. Blend with other ingredients

    Serve cold, as a smoothie, or put in freezer for a few hours. You can add some raisins and nuts before you put it in to freeze.
    Enjoy your ice-cream!

RECIPE #19 Tropical

This is a great recipe to satisfy your sweet tooth!

Serves:1-2

Ingredients:

- 1 mango
- Half a melon
- 1 banana
- 1 kiwi
- Two cups of coconut water
- 1 cup of filtered water
- 1 tablespoon of coconut oil
- A few ice cubes
- A few leaves of fresh mint
- 1 papaya
- Fresh juice of 2 limes

Instructions:

1. Wash the fruits
2. Peal the fruits, and remove the seeds where necessary
3. Squeeze the limes
4. Blend all the ingredients, and add some ice cubes if you want it super cold!

Serve immediately. Garnish with some mint leaves or lime slices.

So delicious!

Much better option than indulging in processed sweets, right?

RECIPE #20 Just Green!

So much is being said about green juices and smoothies. All health watchers talk about it. I think that it's a little bit overhyped. Don't get me wrong, these juices are great for you, but are not always the ultimate cure.

Having said that, I am going to join the green smoothie bandwagon with this recipe!

Serves:1-2

Ingredients:

- One small broccoli, raw or steamed (yes, you will drink it all, you heard me right!)
- One green apple
- A handful of spinach
- A few kale leaves
- 1 kiwi
- 1 teaspoon of powdered chlorella
- A few raisins for taste
- 2 cups of coconut oil water
- Juice of one lemon

Instructions:

1. Wash the broccoli and other ingredients
2. You may want to steam the broccoli slightly and start washing and peeling other ingredients
3. Squeeze the lemon juice
4. When your broccoli is done, cool it down, mix with other ingredients in your blender, and BLEND!

Enjoy the green essence of life!

RECIPE #21 Herbal Smoothie

This smoothie is great for some real Paleo lovers! It is also extremely alkalizing!

Serves: 1-2

Ingredients:

- 2 large tomatoes
- 1 large cucumber
- Half teaspoon tablespoon cilantro
- 2 tablespoons parsley
- 1 teaspoon rosemary
- 1 teaspoon basil
- 2 cloves of garlic
- 1/4 teaspoon cayenne pepper
- Lemon juice of 2 lemons
- Optional: half cup of water

Instructions:

1. Wash and peel the cucumber and tomatoes
2. Squeeze some fresh lemon juice
3. Add the herbs and blend!

Serve immediately; add some ice cubes for extra refreshment. You can garnish it with some fresh mint!

RECIPE #22 Citrus Power!

This is a very quick and nourishing recipe! I love the way citrus flavor is mixed with coconut flavor!

Serves:1

Ingredients:

- 1 large yellow grapefruit
- 1 large green apple
- 1 small lemon
- 1 small orange
- 1 cup of coconut water
- Half cup of coconut milk (optional)

Instructions:

1. Wash and peel the fruits
2. Add some coconut water and coconut milk and blend!
3. Serve immediately!

Enjoy!

Coconut water is a really great ingredient after your workouts! It helps during a post workout recovery.

RECIPE #23 Apple Power!

Apples are perhaps the most popular fruits where I am originally from.

I love them as a quick snack, and I also recognize the fact that they are great for digestion.

And, of course, I use them in my smoothies!

Serves:1-2

Ingredients:

- 3 large apples (green or red)
- Juice of 1 lemon
- 1/2 cup blueberries
- 1/2cup blueberries
- Half cup of coconut water or aloe vera water
- Some cinnamon to spice up
- One small piece of ginger (that in size equals to one garlic clove)

Instructions:

1. Wash and peel the fruits (no need to peel the blueberries, right?)
2. Squeeze some fresh juice of 1 lemon
3. Blend and enjoy!

Aloe vera water is low in calories and high in nutrients and minerals. This is why it is a great ingredient for your smoothies.

This smoothie stimulates digestion and improves micro circulation. If you suffer from water retention, try to drink this smoothie at least 3 times a week.

RECIPE #24 Pear Attack

Here comes another recipe to revitalize and energize. It is low in calories and high in nutrients. Personally, I love blending cucumbers with pears!

Ingredients:

- 1 large red apple
- 2 large green pears
- 1/2 cup fresh cranberries
- 1 stalk celery (large)
- 1 cucumber
- Half cup of coconut water
- One small piece of ginger to taste (you can also use powdered ginger)

Instructions:

1. Wash and peel the fruits.
2. Cut the apple and the pears.
3. Mix with the rest of the ingredients and blend!

Serve immediately! Garnish with a slice of lemon or lime and parsley (Vitamin A!)

RECIPE #25 After Workout Recovery

As I have already mentioned, coconut water helps in post workout recovery and so does the coconut oil. This smoothie is a great mix of sweet coco taste and citrus taste! It's all about finding balance!

Serves:1-2

Ingredients:

- 1 cup prunes (chopped)
- 2 large green pears
- Juice of 1 grapefruit
- Juice of 1 lemon
- 1 tablespoon of coconut oil
- Half cup of coconut water
- 1 stalk celery large

Instructions:

1. Wash the fruits
2. Squeeze some lemon and grapefruit juice
3. Cut the celery and pears
4. Mix with the rest of the ingredients and blend.

Serve immediately!

Have a nice post-workout recovery!

RECIPE #26 Veggies Are Awesome!

I think that some people prefer drinking veggies to eating them. It's so much easier! Join the club with this green recipe!

Serves:1

Ingredients:

- 1 cup of spinach leaves
- Half cup of romaine lettuce leaves
- 1 celery stalk
- 1 small red apple
- 1 cucumber
- Half cup of almond milk

Instructions:

1. Wash the spinach, apple and lettuce
2. Peel the apple and cucumber. Cut into small pieces. Cut the celery stalk
3. Blend with other ingredients.

Serve immediately,

Enjoy!

RECIPE #27 Naturopathy Rocks: Liver Detox 1

This is a great recipe to take care of your liver and give you more energy.

I suggest you do it in the morning, before breakfast, for about 30 days. Of course, for a more specific treatment, you would need to contact your naturopathic doctor or practitioner. I am just telling you how I do it.

The best seasons to cleanse your liver are springtime and autumn.

Ingredients:

- 2 cups of warm water
- 3 fresh lemons
- 1 grapefruit
- 1 clove of garlic
- A few leaves of baby spinach
- 1 cucumber
- 1 tablespoon of flaxseed oil
- 3-4 fresh mint leaves
- 2 pinches of cumin
- 1 teaspoon of some grated ginger root

Instructions:

1. Wash the fruits and vegetables, peel and chop.
2. Squeeze the lemon and grapefruit juice
3. Peel and cut the cucumber and garlic
4. Mix all the ingredients in a blender, then add some flaxseed oil, and stir for about a minute. Enjoy!

RECIPE #28 Naturopathy Rocks: Liver Detox 2

Here comes the second option of the previous recipe.

Ingredients:

- Juice of 1 lemon
- 2 apples, sliced and seeded
- 1 tablespoon of virgin olive oil
- Handful of grapes
- 1 small piece of ginger (size of a garlic clove)
- 1 cup of water
- Half teaspoon of powdered chlorella

Instructions:

1. Wash the ingredients
2. Squeeze the lemon juice
3. Mix with the rest of the ingredients, and add some chlorella powder.
4. Blend and enjoy. Happy liver!

RECIPE #29 Green But Sweet!

If you want to introduce your kids to green smoothies, check out this recipe! It is sweet actually. Yes!

This recipe serves 2-3. It makes sure that parents also go green smoothing! After all, who should set an example...?

Ingredients:

- 1 ripe mango
- 2 bananas
- 1 cup of baby spinach
- 1 teaspoon of spiruline powder
- 2 cups of water (you can add some lemon juice to taste)
- 1 cup of coconut water
- 1 cup fresh parsley
- 2 green apples
- 8 date fruits

Instructions:

1. Wash and peel the fruits.
2. Squeeze some lemon juice if you want to add it to your smoothie
3. Mix all the ingredients; add some spiruline powder and a few date fruits, depending on how sweet you want your smoothie to be!

Enjoy! You can sprinkle some cacao powder to make it even more inviting!

RECIPE #30 Easy Weight Loss

This smoothie is great to stimulate your metabolism and help you lose weight.

Make sure you drink it on a regular basis. It is a low calorie recipe and really energizing and refreshing. All you need when undergoing a weight loss regime!

Serves:1

Ingredients:

- 1 cup of spinach leaves
- 1 cup of arugula
- 1 carrot
- 1 beetroot
- One tablespoon of oat bran
- Juice of two grapefruits
- Water (if necessary), or even better aloe vera water or coconut oil water

Instructions:

1. Wash the ingredients and peel them.
2. Cut the carrot and the beetroot.
3. Squeeze the grapefruit juice

Blend and enjoy!

Serve with some fresh parsley, mint, and a slice of lime!

RECIPE #31 Alkaline Batteries

Do you want to get your alkaline batteries recharged?

Here are the ingredients:

- 2 carrots
- 1 apple
- 2 cucumbers
- 1 small piece of ginger (1 tablespoon of powdered ginger)
- 1 lime (with skin-must be organic)
- 1 Tablespoon Wheat Grass
- 1/2 cup of filtered water
- Juice of one lemon
- Half teaspoon of powdered almonds
- Half teaspoon of powdered chlorella

Instructions:
1. Wash and peel the fruit and veg.
2. Squeeze the lemon juice and mix with some water
3. Mix with the rest of the ingredients
4. Blend and enjoy!

Garnish with some fresh mint and parsley.

Serves:2

Apples and carrots are an excellent combination. It is said to prevent cancer and other diseases. I suggest you research Doctor Gerson's therapy if you are interested in finding out all the benefits that such a simple blend can bring.

RECIPE #32 Sweet Again!

Here comes some nice, natural refreshment for the summer!

Natural sweet is always better than artificial, chemical sweet, right?

Serves:1

Ingredients:

- 1 banana,
- 4 date fruits (remove the seed)
- 1 cup almond milk,
- tablespoon maple syrup,
- 1 tablespoon cinnamon
- 5 ice cubes
- One tablespoon of powdered chlorella
- Half teaspoon of soy lecithin

Instructions:

1. Wash and peel the banana
2. Mix with other ingredients and the ice cubes
3. Blend and enjoy!

RECIPE #33 Macrobiotic Summer

This smoothie is energizing and a natural aphrodisiac. Use with caution!

Serves: 1-2

Ingredients:

- 5 dried apricots
- 1 cup of strawberries
- Half 1 teaspoon of maca powder
- Half-cup of cooked brown rice (can be also some cooked quinoa in the same amount)
- Half teaspoon of cinnamon
- 1 banana
- 1 apple (green or red)
- 1 tablespoon of coconut oil

Instructions:
1. Wash the ingredients (when necessary), peel and cut into pieces
2. Add half teaspoon of maca powder (super aphrodisiac, be careful!)
3. Blend and enjoy!

RECIPE #34 Mediterranean Recipe

This is a really simple and easy to make recipe inspired by the Mediterranean cuisine! I love the original, fresh Greek yogurt in my smoothies. This ingredient can also be replaced, if for some reason, you don't eat yoghurt.

Serves:2

Ingredients:

- 2 avocados

- 2 Greek yogurts (if you are vegan, or Paleo, you can replace it with some coconut milk or rice milk. I have also tried soy yogurts with this one, good for vegans, but of course, off the Paleo Diet).

- 1 cucumber

- 2 leaves of mint

-1 pinch of black pepper

-1 big apple

-1 pinch of Himalayan sat

Instructions:

1. Wash the apple, the cucumber, and the avocado. Peel them.
2. Cut into small pieces and mix with the rest of the ingredients
3. Blend and enjoy!

Serve as a smoothie or as a super refreshing dip, for example, with some raw veggies (carrots, cucumbers, tomatoes)

RECIPE #35 VITAMIN STRAWBERRY SMOOTHIE

Another super delicious recipe for smoothie warriors!

Serves:1

Ingredients:

- 1 banana
- 3 slices of fresh pineapple
- 1 cup of fresh orange juice
- 1 lemon
- 1 cup of rice milk
- 2 tablespoons wheat germ
- 1 tablespoon of honey
- Some currants and mint leaves to garnish

Instructions:

1. Wash the fruits
2. Squeeze some lemon juice (1 lemon is enough) and orange juice (1 orange)
3. Blend with other ingredients. Garnish with some fresh mint leaves and currants. Serve immediately!

   Enjoy!

RECIPE #36 Easy and Relaxing!

Are you looking for some original smoothie refreshment?

Try this one; your body will be grateful!

Serves:2

Ingredients:

- 1 cup of chopped lettuce leaves
- 1 cup of spinach leaves
- 1 cup of orange juice
- Half cup of water
- Two stalks of celery
- A few ice cubes
- 1 pinch of cinnamon
- Optional: 1 pinch of Himalayan salt
- About 2 square cms of alga dry wakame

Instructions:

1. Soak alga wakame in some filtered, cold water. Leave in for about 15 minutes.
2. Squeeze some fresh orange juice, and mix with water
3. Wash other ingredients and chop finely (check your blender for preferences; like I said in the intro, my old blender went on an early retirement plan...!)
4. Mix with other ingredients, including some soaked alga, blend and enjoy!

RECIPE #37 Sweet Again!!!

I really recommend this recipe for students! All you need to get your focus energy back!

Ingredients (for 4 students...!)

- 4 bananas,
- 2 big, ripe avocadoes
- Four tablespoons of organic honey
- 4 glasses of vegan milk
- Some grated nuts(for example almond powder)
- 10 raising
- 2 tablespoons of lecithin granules
- 1 teaspoon of spiruline powder

Instructions:

1. Wash the bananas and avocados, cut into pieces
2. Mix with the rest of the ingredients, blend and enjoy!

If you find it too sweet, add some lime or lemon juice.

Garnish with powdered cinnamon and cacao!

RECIPE #38 Super Relaxing!

Do you really feel like you need to unwind and relax? Have you had a bad day at work?

Try this recipe!

Serves:1

Ingredients:

- 1 cup of cooled valerian infusion
- 3 slices of pineapple
- 1 avocado
- 1 teaspoon of soy lecithin
- 1 teaspoon of organic honey or coconut oil
- 1 cup of almond milk or rice milk

Instructions:

1. Wash and peel the avocado (remove the seed) and pineapple. Slice them.
2. Mix with other ingredients and blend. Then, add one teaspoon of coconut oil or organic honey, and stir for about 1 minute.
3. Serve immediately, relax and enjoy!

RECIPE#39 Herbal Taste Smoothie!

Ok, you may know that fucus infusion is good for you, but its taste is not the best, really! This is why I like to use it for smoothies as I can transform its taste.

Fucus is great for anti-cellulite treatments, detoxification, and water retention.

Serves:1-2

Ingredients:

- 1 cup of cooled fucus infusion (1 teabag)
- 3 slices of pineapples
- 2 peaches, peeled (remove the seed)
- Half mango
- Juice of 1 lemon
- 1 tablespoon of organic honey

Instructions:

1. Wash and peel the peaches and the pineapple, cut into small pieces.
2. Mix with 1 cup of cooled focus infusion, and add some lemon juice. Blend.
3. Add one teaspoon of organic honey
4. Serve immediately! This smoothie is great to fight food cravings!

RECIPE#40 Anti-cough, Anti-cold

This recipe is great to naturally strengthen your immune system.

Serves:1-2

Ingredients:

- 1 cup of cooled rosemary infusion
- Juice of 2 lemons
- 2 kiwis
- 2 apples
- 1 garlic clove
- 1 teaspoon of dried rosemary herb
- 1 teaspoon of powdered ginger

Instructions:

1. Prepare 1 cup of rosemary infusion and cool down
2. Squeeze the lemon juice
3. Wash and peel the kiwis and the apples
4. Blend all the ingredients, add some rosemary herb and ginger powder.

Enjoy! There is no time to get sick, life is too good!

RECIPE#41 Low Calorie and Refreshing

This is an excellent smoothie for those who are on weight loss regimes and wish to prevent food cravings. Mint is a wonderful solution! Especially when you drink it in a smoothie that is also rich in vitamins and minerals and tastes nice!

Serves:1

Ingredients:

- 1 cup of cooled mint infusion (optional- you can mix it with some green tea)
- 1 kiwi
- Half cucumber
- 1 red apple
- A few slices of pineapple
- 1 teaspoon of coconut oil

Instructions:

1. Prepare the mint infusion.
2. Wash and peel the kiwi, cucumber, pineapple, etc. Cut into small pieces.
3. Blend all the ingredients. Finally, add one tea spoon of coconut oil.
4. Stir for about a minute.
5. Serve immediately. Garnish with a slice of lime!

RECIPE#42 High Calorie and Energetic

This is a smoothie recipe for those who, like me, don't count calories.

It is extremely nutritious, and I recommend it for busy and active days or strenuous workouts!

Serves:1-2

Ingredients:

- 2 bananas
- 1 big avocado
- 2 tablespoons of organic peanut butter or almond butter
- Juice of 2 lemons
- 1 tablespoon of coconut oil
- 1 cup of almond milk
- 1 cup of strawberries
- 1 teaspoon of soy lecithin
- A handful of raisins + a few date fruits
- A few leaves of spinach
- 1 teaspoon of spiruline

Instructions:

1. Wash and peel the ingredients when necessary.
2. Squeeze the juice of 2 lemons.
3. Mix with other ingredients and blend.
4. Serve immediately and enjoy your active day!

RECIPE#43 Spicy

A friend of mine tried my apple-carrot-cucumber juice, and she did not like it.

This is why I decided to spice it up!

Check out this recipe, it's great as an aperitif!

Serves:1-2

Ingredients:

- 4 carrots
- 2 red apples
- 1 cucumber
- Juice of one lemon
- Half a cup of water (optional)
- 1 pinch of Himalayan salt
- Tiny bit of chili powder (Ok, it's up to you, but be careful!)
- Half onion
- 1 garlic clove
- 1 tablespoon of virgin olive oil or coconut oil

OPTIONAL: add some broccoli, and make it a super alkaline killer!

This smoothie is really alkalizing and detoxifying, and at the same time, it has a really unique taste!

Instructions:

1. Wash and peel the fruits and veggies.
2. Squeeze some lemon juice.

3. Mix with other ingredients and blend. Add some salt and chili powder, and stir.

Serve slightly chilled, or with some ice cubes. You may add some vinegar or lime juice for more taste.

RECIPE#44 Simple Paleo Smoothie

This is an excellent smoothie for Paleo fans!

Serves:1

Ingredients:

- 1 cup of blueberries
- 1 avocado
- 1 kiwi
- 1 cup of coconut milk (hazelnut or almond milk is also fine)
- 2 egg whites
- Some Ice (optional)

Instructions:

1. Wash and peel the ingredients when necessary
2. Blend and enjoy!
3. Serve with a slice of lemon or lime.Enjoy!

RECIPE#45 Sweet ROCKS!

If you crave for something sweet and healthy, you have just found the solution!

Serves:1-2

Ingredients:

- 2 peeled kiwis
- 2 medium bananas
- 1 cup low almond milk
- 1 teaspoon of honey
- 1 tablespoon of coconut milk to taste
- A few raisins
- 1 teaspoon cinnamon
- 1 teaspoon cacao powder
- 1 teaspoon sesame

Instructions:

1. Wash and peel the fruits
2. Mix with other ingredients, and blend!
3. Serve with some ice cubes, and sprinkle over some cacao powder and sesame!

Enjoy!

RECIPE#46 Sesame Dream

This smoothie will restore your energy levels sooner than you expect!

Serves:1

Ingredients:

- 1 avocado, pitted
- 1 cup of spinach leaves
- 1 cup of almond milk
- 1 tablespoon of sesame
- A few strawberries
- A few pineapple chunks

Instructions:

1. Wash and peel the fruits. Chop.
2. Mix with other ingredients, and blend.
3. Serve with a slice of lime or lemon!

Enjoy!

RECIPE#47 More Sesame

Here comes another energizing sesame seeds smoothie!

Serves:1-2

Ingredients:

- 2 peaches
- 2 carrots
- 2 apples
- Half cup of water
- Juice of 2 grapefruits
- 1 tablespoon of powdered sesame seeds
- Half teaspoon of powdered chlorella or spiruline
- Optional: a few tablespoons of coconut milk to taste

Instructions:

1. Wash, peel, and chop the fruits.
2. Squeeze some grapefruit fruits.
3. Mix with other ingredients and blend.
4. Add some powdered sesame seeds and powdered chlorella (or spiruline).
5. Add some coconut milk, and stir.

Serve immediately! Enjoy!

RECIPE#48 Quinoa and Brown Rice Mix

This is an excellent breakfast recipe. Not suitable for hardcore Paleo's though. Unless...they want to try it...

I love nourishing my body with natural foods, and I know that quinoa and brown rice are good carbs. This is why I include them in my smoothies! Join me, and you will understand what I mean.

Serves:1-2

Ingredients:

- Half cup of cooked quinoa
- Half cup of brown rice
- Half cup of water
- Half cup of almond milk
- A few strawberries or blueberries or...whatever fruit you can find in your kitchen (make it freestyle!)
- Half teaspoon cinnamon

Instructions:

1. Wash the strawberries (or blueberries)
2. Blend with other ingredients
3. Add some cinnamon, and stir energetically
4. Enjoy your smoothie!

RECIPE#49 Amaranth Smoothie

This recipe is a bit similar to the previous one.

Amaranth is also a good source of good carbs. It is rich in iron and magnesium, and I love it in my smoothies.

This smoothie is inspired by the macrobiotic diet. Paleo fans may not like it though.

However, like I said in the intro, if you want to make it strictly paleo, just replace amaranth grains with some kind of fruit or vegetables that your taste buds like.

This is an example of a nice, alkaline and balanced breakfast. Perfect for Alkaline Diet Lovers who don't want to go hungry or survive on steamed broccoli only...

Serves:1-2

Ingredients:

- Half cup of amaranth grain
- 1 cup of filtered water
- Half cup of rice milk or almond milk
- About 3 square cms of dry alga wakame
- 2 carrots
- 1 apple
- Juice of 1 lemon
- 1 teaspoon cinnamon

Instructions:

1. Soak alga wakame in cold water (filtered), cover and leave for about 15 minutes

2. In the meantime, wash the amaranth and put it to boil (mix a cup of water with half cup of almond milk or rice milk). Use low heat.
3. Wash and peel the carrots and apple. Cut into small pieces and add to boiling amaranth.
4. Add some cinnamon. When the amaranth is done, stop the heat.
5. Let it cool down, add some lemon juice and alga wakame, and blend. In the winter, I like it slightly warm. In the summer, I cool it down and add some ice cubes.

Enjoy the Macrobiotic-Alkaline way! I do!

RECIPE#50 Millet Detox Smoothie

Here comes a really simple, yet extremely nutritious, smoothie recipe. If you happen to have any millet leftovers, use it for your smoothie!

Serves:1-2

Ingredients:

- Half cup of cooked millet
- Half teaspoon of powdered ginger
- Half teaspoon cinnamon
- 2 apples
- 1 cup of almond milk or rice milk
- A few blueberries to out on top

Instructions:

1. Wash, peel, and cut the apples
2. Mix with other ingredients and blend
3. Add cinnamon powder and ginger powder, and stir.
4. Add some blueberries.

You can serve it immediately or cool id down. It's really great as a dessert.

RECIPE#51 Fat Burner

Are you wanting to burn some fat?

Make sure you drink this smoothie on a regular basis!

Serves:1

Ingredients:

- 1 cup of Chinese red tea (1 teabag)
- 1 cup of blueberries
- Juice of 2 lemons
- 1 apple
- A few pineapple slices
- A few raisins

Instructions:

1. Prepare 1 cup of red tea, and let it cool down (you may add some ice cubes to speed it up).
2. Squeeze the lemon juice
3. Wash and peel other ingredients.
4. Blend and enjoy!

Drink it once a day or at least 3 times per week.

RECIPE #52 Coffee Lovers

Some people just can't imagine skipping their morning coffee, yet, they always skip proper breakfast. Here's the solution, a quick, 2 in one smoothie that also contains some coffee.

Remember: coffee is extremely acidic, and so is the cow's milk.

However, you can at least try to neutralize coffee's acidity by adding some almond milk and a few pieces of fruit that will give you some fiber and energy.

If you want to quit coffee, then I suggest you make it weaker and weaker every time. You will finally realize that you are making a really healthy transition—from coffee to smoothie..!

Serves: 1

Ingredients:

- Half cup of cooled organic coffee (don't make it too strong)
- Half cup of almond milk
- Half teaspoon of cinnamon
- 1 banana (it will help you prevent the midday food cravings)
- A few strawberries
- One apple

Instructions:

1. Prepare some coffee, and let it cool down.
2. Take about half cup of coffee and mix it with some almond milk
3. Wash and peel the fruits
4. Mix all the ingredients and blend.
5. Enjoy your 2 in 1 smoothie!

After all, it's all about your real energy. You want to be bouncing off the walls!

If you don't feel hungry in the morning, try to have a smoothie. Or this one, or whichever you feel like having. The worst thing that you can do is to skip breakfast because, in the morning, your body needs some nutrients to feel vibrant and energetic. If you skip breakfast, you can also feel moody and tired around midday. Add to it: some uncontrolled food cravings...we don't want to be there, do we..?

Conclusion

I hope that my booklet gave you some nice smoothie recipes ideas. I really want to encourage you to start now and revitalize your body and mind.

A healthy and vibrant body and a focused mind are waiting for you!

Preparing your smoothies will be the best time investment you can possibly make.

I also suggest you start considering your local organic option. I can't give you any specific tips here as different countries and regions have different prices and rules. A few years ago, I thought that organic fruits and veggies were very extremely expensive. Ok, it's the truth, I spend more money on organic foods, but to be honest, the difference is not that much. I just found some really good local organic providers, and I usually make an order with some neighbors and friends, this is why it is much cheaper. I also visit my local market regularly, and therefore, do not need to shop at my local supermarket. Organic tastes better.

Do your own research and at least try to shop organic whenever you can.

About 50 years ago, everything used to be organic. It's sad what's happening now. They make us pay more for real foods!

It's also worth mentioning that if more and more people shopped organic, the prices would drop.

REMEMBER TO GRAB YOUR FREE COMPLIMENTARY eBook:

Join my wellness + holistic lifestyle design newsletter and get free instant
access to my guide: "Revolutionize Your Life with Alkaline Foods" + my insider news, amazing
free bonuses + receive all my upcoming books for free or 99c.
Start creating a happy body, mind and spirit today!

Subscribe here:
www.HolisticWellnessProject.com/alkaline

If you happen to have any problems with your free download, let us know:

info@holisticwellnessproject.com

I NEED YOUR HELP!

Finally, if you liked my book, please post a review on Amazon.

"Please, please, make Marta's day, and leave an honest review! We live with her and we support her; we know how much time and effort she puts into her writing. Let us know what you think.

We always review her books at Amazon. Meow !

Cheers and Meow. Wellness, we know it! , xxx Marta's cats: Uacia and Mauek "

****

If you happen to have any questions, doubts, or suggestions, please send me an e-mail: info@holisticwellnessproject.com

For more inspiration and empowerment visit:

www.holisticwellnessproject.com

You will find all my books both in kindle and paperback (nutrition, wellness, motivation, spirituality, holistic lifestyle, personal development) at:

www.bitly.com/MartaBooks

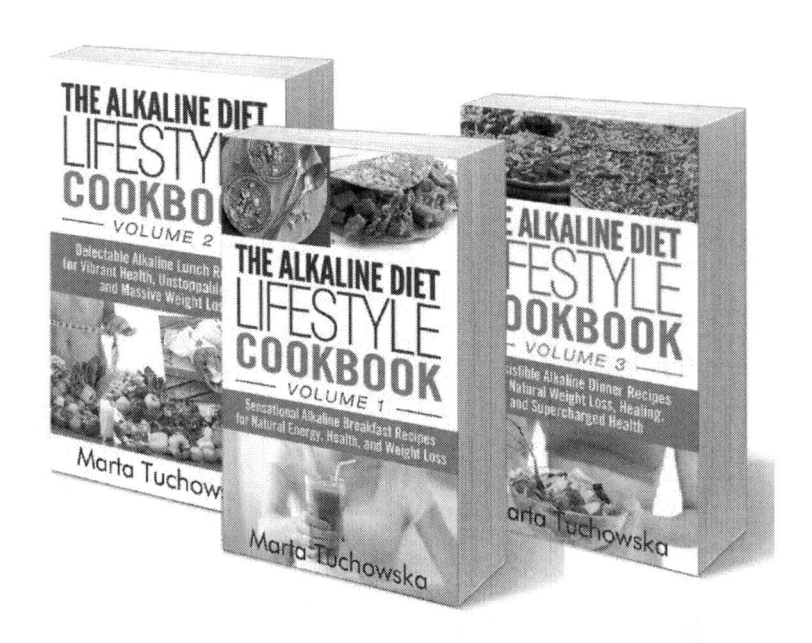

Don't forget to follow me on Instagram. You'll get your daily wellness, health and fitness inspiration + much, much more!

www.instagram.com/marta_wellness

You can also connect with me at:

www.facebook.com/HolisticWellnessProject

www.pinterest.com/MartaWellness

www.plus.google.com/+MartaTuchowska

www.twitter.com/Marta_Wellness

ABOUT MARTA TUCHOWSKA

Marta is a certified massage therapist, wellness/lifestyle coach and author dedicated to helping others transform their bodies and minds to achieve personal success. Her passion for holistic wellness and personal development led her to study holistic nutrition, NLP, yoga, meditation, reiki, stress management, alkaline diet, aromatherapy, herbal remedies and homeopathy. She became fascinated with the power of the mind as well as motivational "action" coaching.

She believes that natural therapies and personal growth are a life-long study and she never stops investigating.

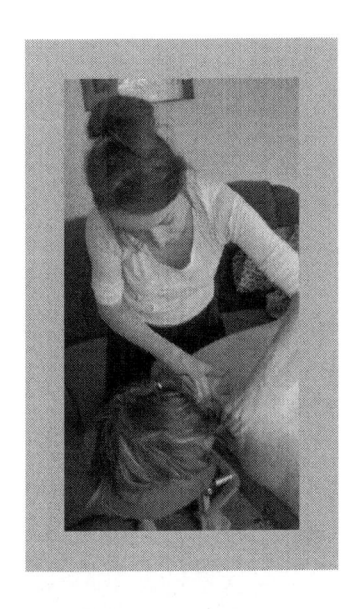

"GLOBAL HOLISTIC WELLNESS COACHING FOR MODERN PEOPLE..."

Marta realized early on that wellness is not only about taking care of your body. She chose to expand her services from simple massage to offering a more holistic approach to wellness, lifestyle coaching and alternative services. Marta truly believes that if you really want to transform yourself in a holistic way, you must also work on your mind, emotions and motivation. All systems must go - body, mind and spirit.

Marta is a seeker, a researcher and a holistic warrior. It's all about changing your mindset! This concept led to the creation of Marta's Motivational Holistic Wellness Coaching for Modern People. The origins of Marta's first motivational book, "Committed to Wellness", stems from her fascination with holistic wellness and personal development, her first-hand knowledge and intense study of the power of change, and her passion for sharing the techniques that are now helping people all over the world to change their own mindset about fitness and nutrition.

NATURAL BENEFITS.
Marta knows firsthand the power of natural therapies. The reason is very simple: When she was five years old, Marta suffered from severe attacks of uveitis and nearly lost her eyesight. Chemical medical treatments only made her poor, weak system out of balance and no traditional medicines seemed to work. The doctors at that time did not know how to cure uveitis. Luckily, her parents searched for other solutions and they found a medical doctor who also specialized in naturopathy. It was thanks to homeopathy, phytotherapy and balanced nutrition that uveitis attacks were defeated and her eyesight was saved. The doctor that saved her eyesight is now almost 100 years old and is still enjoying great health! Every day she is grateful that natural medicine has provided her with solutions. This is why she is such a believer in natural medicine.

To clarify, as a patient, Marta also believes in traditional medicine and the fusion of the two worlds, but she always advises people to explore the natural and holistic ways as much as possible.

HOLISTIC TRANSFORMATION...
At 31, Marta feels focused, happy and fulfilled. Of course, she had her ups and downs on her way to discovering her passion and her way, but she also feels grateful for bad times. She recognizes the fact that it is thanks to obstacles that we grow and push ourselves to think outside of the box (yes, the famous BOX!). Marta herself struggled with the lack of purpose and no zest for life for some time, those negative experiences actually served her well as a catalyst to her discovery of the world of Natural Therapies and WELLNESS.

Printed in Great Britain
by Amazon